R&B SONGS FOR UKULELE

ISBN 978-1-4950-9570-2

7777 W. BLUEMOUND RD. P.O. BOX 13819 MILWAUKEE, WI 53213

Visit Hal Leonard Online at
www.halleonard.com

Ain't No Sunshine

Words and Music by Bill Withers

Brick House

Words and Music by Lionel Richie, Ronald LaPread, Walter Orange,
Milan Williams, Thomas McClary and William King

brick house. ___ Ow, that la-dy's stacked ___ and that's a fact, ___

ain't hold-in' noth-in' back. ___ Oh, she's a brick ___ house, ___ yeah. ___

She's the one, ___ the on-ly one, ___ built like an Am-a-zon. ___

Verse

2. The clothes she wear, ___ her sex-y ways ___ make an

old ___ man ___ wish for young-er days, ___ yeah, yeah.

She knows she's built and knows how to please. _

Sho' nuf can knock a strong _ man to his knees, _ 'cause she's a

Outro-Chorus

Am   Bm   Am   Bm   Am   Bm

brick   house. _⎫
Brick   house. _⎭   Yeah, _ she's might-y, might-y, _ just

Am   Bm   Am   Bm   Am   Bm

let-tin' it all _ hang out. _ Ah, she's a   brick   house. _   ⎰That
                                                                                ⎱Yeah,

Am   Bm   Am   Bm   Am

la - dy's stacked _ and that's a fact, _ ain't hold-in' noth-in' back. _ Ow!
she's the one, _ the on - ly one, _ built like an Am - a - zon. _ Yeah!

(Sittin' On)
The Dock of the Bay

Words and Music by Steve Cropper and Otis Redding

Oo, __ I'm just sit - tin' on the dock of the bay, __ wast - in' time. __

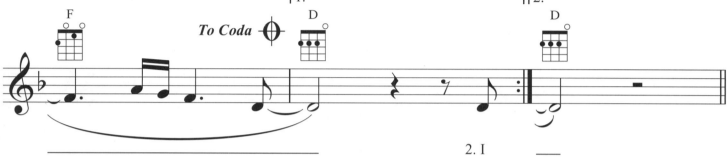

2. I

Bridge

Look like noth-in's gon - na change; ___ ev - 'ry-thing

still re-mains the same. _ I can't do what ten peo-ple tell me ___ to do, __

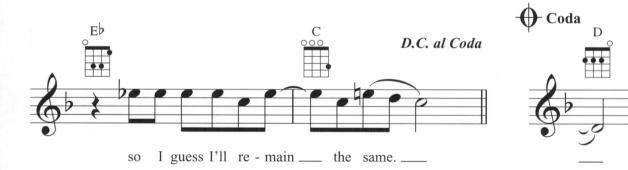

so I guess I'll re - main ___ the same. ___ ___ (Whistling)

Outro

Repeat and fade

Heatwave
(Love Is Like a Heatwave)

Words and Music by Edward Holland, Lamont Dozier and Brian Holland

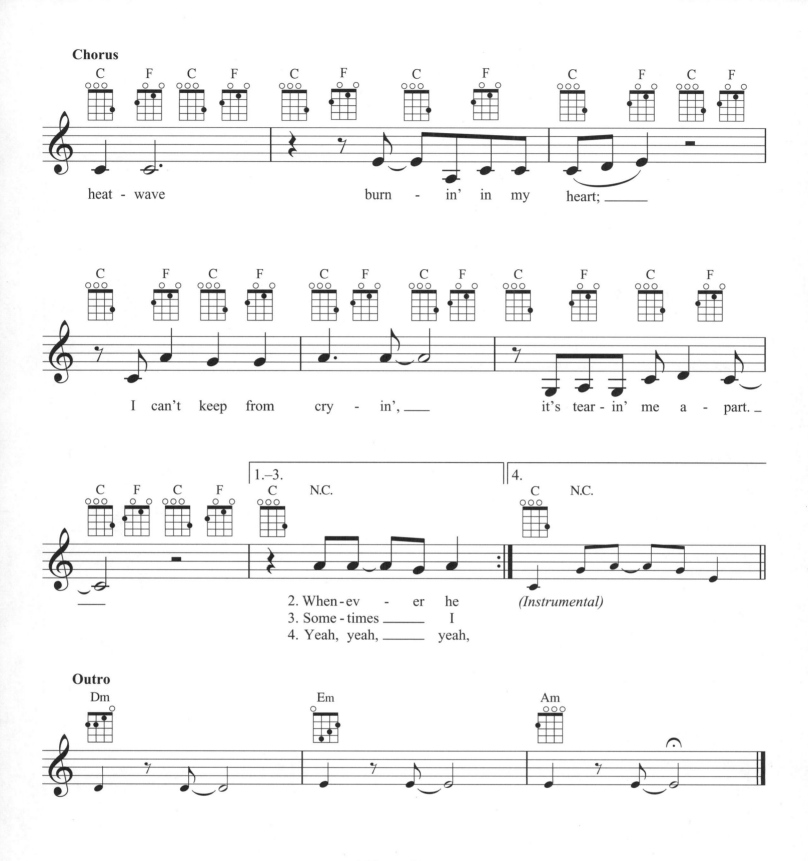

Additional Lyrics

2. Whenever he calls my name, soft, low, sweet and plain,
   I feel, yeah yeah, well, I feel that burnin' flame.
   Has high blood pressure got a hold on me
   Or is this the way love's supposed to be?

3. Sometimes I stare into space, tears all over my face;
   I can't explain it, don't understand it.
   I ain't never felt like this before.
   Now that funny feelin' has me amazed;
   I don't know what to do, my head's in a haze.

4. Yeah, yeah, yeah, yeah, yeah, yeah, whoa ho.
   Yeah, yeah, yeah, yeah, ho.
   Don't pass up this chance,
   This time it's a true romance.

How Sweet It Is
(To Be Loved by You)

Words and Music by Edward Holland, Lamont Dozier and Brian Holland

Pre-Chorus

Chorus

1., 2.

3.

Outro-Chorus

Repeat and fade

with sweet love and de - vo - tion,
But you bright - en up for me all of my days —
You were bet - ter to me than I was to my - self; — for

deep - ly touch - ing my e - mo - tion. —
with a love so sweet in so man - y ways. — } I want to
me there's — you and there ain't no - bod - y else. —

stop and thank you, ba - by; I want — to stop and thank you,

ba - by. How sweet it is ____ to be loved by you.

How sweet it is ____ to be loved by you.

How sweet it is ____ to be loved by you.

I Can't Help Myself
(Sugar Pie, Honey Bunch)

Words and Music by Brian Holland, Lamont Dozier and Edward Holland Jr.

Verse
Moderately fast

1. Sug - ar pie, hon - ey bunch, you know that I
3. sug - ar pie, hon - ey bunch, I'm weak - er than a

love you. ___ I can't help my - self,
man should be. I can't help my - self,

I love ___ you and no - bod - y else. ___
I'm a ___ fool in love, you see. ___ Wan-na tell ___

In and out my life, you come and you go, ___
___ you I don't love you, tell ___ you that we're through.

___ And I've tried, ___ leav - ing just your pic - ture be - hind, ___
but ev - 'ry time I see your face, ___

and I kissed it a thou - sand times. __   2. When __

I get all __ choked up __ in - side. __   4. When __

Verse

__ you snap your fin - ger or wink your eye, __ I come a -

run -ning to you. __   I'm tied __ to your a - pron strings __

and there's noth - ing __ that I can do. __ *(Instrumental)*

Interlude

Can't

help my - self, __ no, __ I can't help my - self.   'cause,

D.C. al Coda

17

I Heard It Through the Grapevine

Words and Music by Norman J. Whitfield and Barrett Strong

prise, _____ I must say, _____ when I found out yes - ter - day. _

Chorus

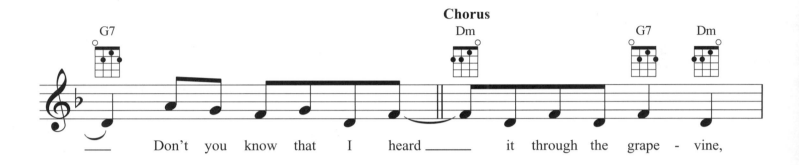

_____ Don't you know that I heard _____ it through the grape - vine,

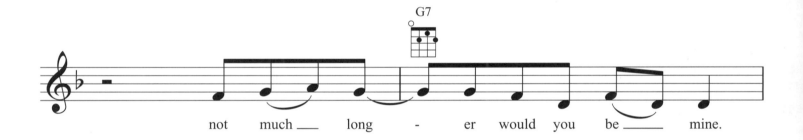

not much ___ long - er would you be ___ mine.

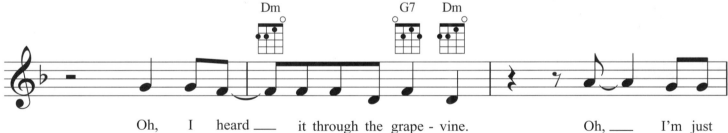

Oh, I heard ___ it through the grape - vine. Oh, ___ I'm just

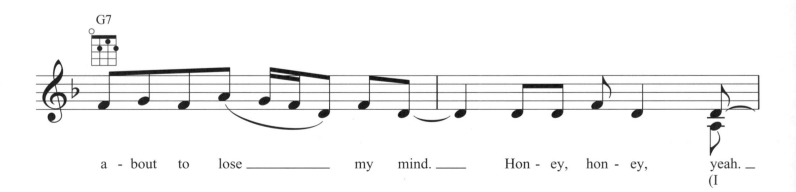

a - bout to lose _____ my mind. ___ Hon - ey, hon - ey, yeah. _
(I

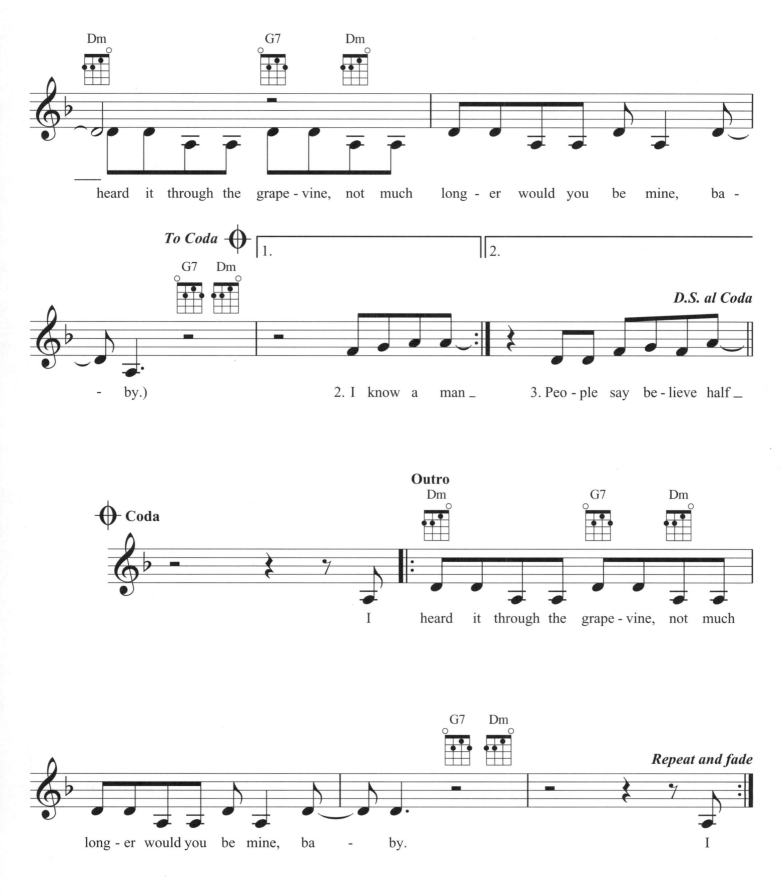

Additional Lyrics

2. I know a man ain't supposed to cry,
   But these tears I can't hold inside.
   Losing you would end my life, you see,
   'Cause you mean that much to me.
   You could have told me yourself
   That you loved someone else.
   Instead, I heard...

3. People say believe half of what you see,
   Oh, and none of what you hear.
   But I can't help but be confused.
   If it's true, please tell me, dear.
   Do you plan to let me go
   For the other guy you loved before?
   Don't you know I heard...

I Just Called to Say I Love You

Words and Music by Stevie Wonder

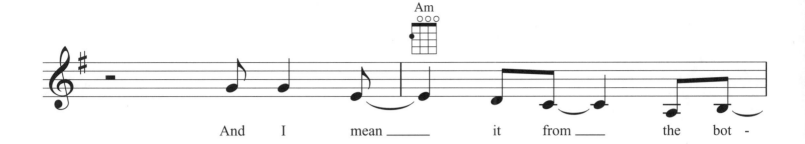

And I mean _____ it from _____ the bot -

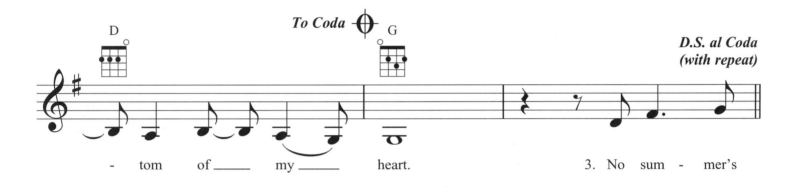

- tom of _____ my _____ heart.   3. No sum - mer's

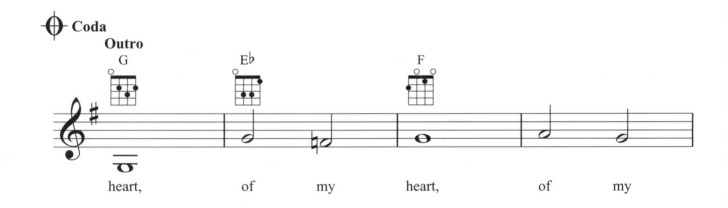

heart,   of   my   heart,   of   my

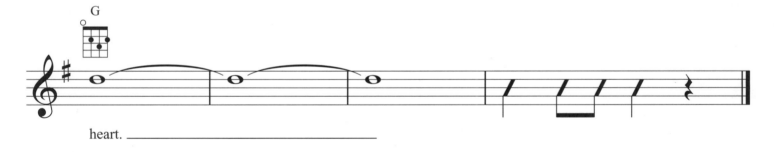

heart. _____

Additional Lyrics

3. No summer's high, no warm July,
   No harvest moon to light one tender August night.
   No autumn breeze, no falling leaves,
   Not even time for birds to fly to southern skies.

4. No Libra sun, no Halloween,
   No giving thanks to all the Christmas joy you bring.
   But what it is, though old so new,
   To fill your heart like no three words could ever do.

I'll Be There

Words and Music by Berry Gordy Jr., Hal Davis, Willie Hutch and Bob West

In the Midnight Hour

Words and Music by Steve Cropper and Wilson Pickett

Just Once

Words by Cynthia Weil
Music by Barry Mann

make the mag - ic last ___ for more ___ than just one ___ night? ___ If

1.

we could just ___ get to ___ it, I know we could ___ break through it.

Bridge

2.

we could just ___ get to ___ it. Just _____ once, I want to

un - der - stand ___ why it al - ways ___ comes back ___ to good -

bye. _____ Why _____ can't we get our - selves in hand ___

and ad - mit to one an - oth - er we're no good with - out ___ each oth - er?

Chorus

Additional Lyrics

2. I gave my all, but I think my all may have been too much,
   'Cause Lord knows we're not getting anywhere.
   It seems we're always blowin' whatever we've got goin',
   And it seems at times, with all we've got, we haven't got a prayer.

Chorus: Just once, can't we figure out what we keep doin' wrong,
   Why the good times never last for long?
   Where are we goin' wrong?
   Just once, can't we find a way to finally make it right,
   To make the magic last for more than just one night?
   I know we could break through it if we could just get to it.

Lean on Me

Words and Music by Bill Withers

I'll help you car - ry ___ on; _____

for ___ it won't be long _____ 'til I'm gon - na need __

___ some - bod - y to lean _____ on. ___

Verse

2. Please _____ swal - low your pride _____ if I have things __
3. If _____ there is a load _____ you have to bear __

___ you need to bor - row, _____
that you can't car - ry, _____

for ___ no one can fill _____ those of your needs __
I'm ___ right up the road. _____ I'll share your load __

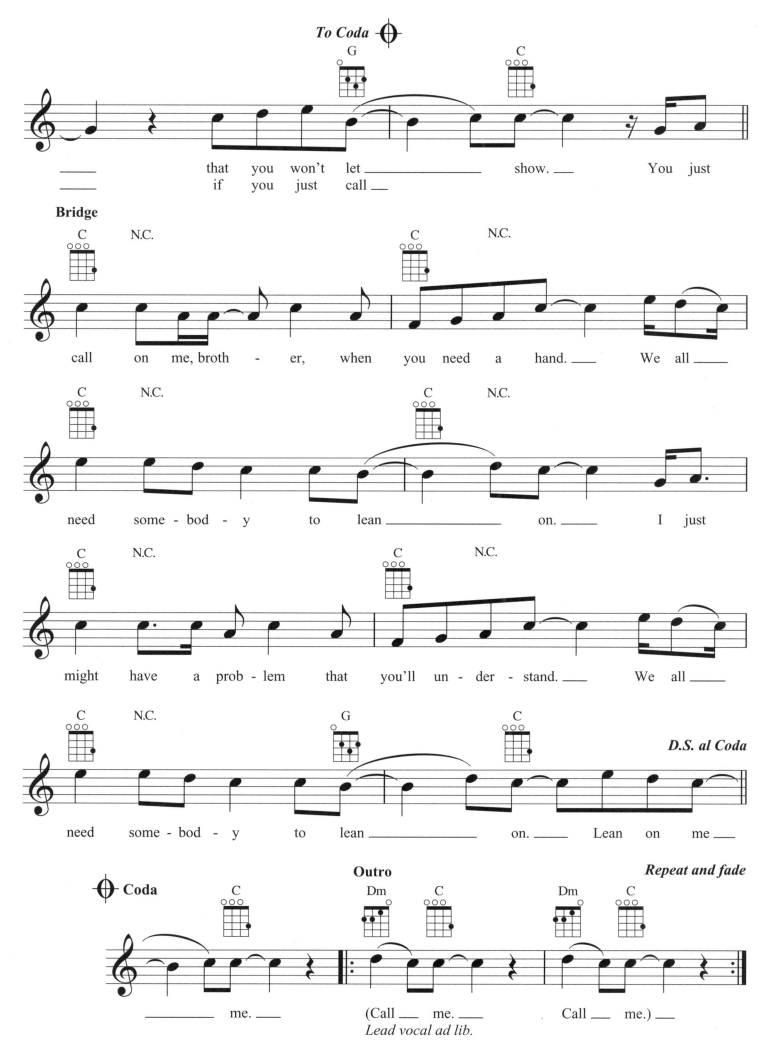

My Girl

Words and Music by Smokey Robinson and Ronald White

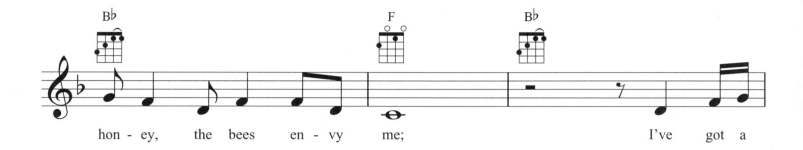

hon - ey, the bees en - vy me; I've got a

sweet - er song _____ than the birds in the tree. Well,

Chorus

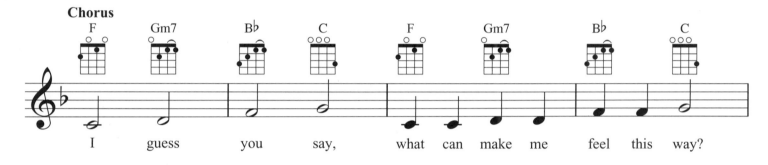

I guess you say, what can make me feel this way?

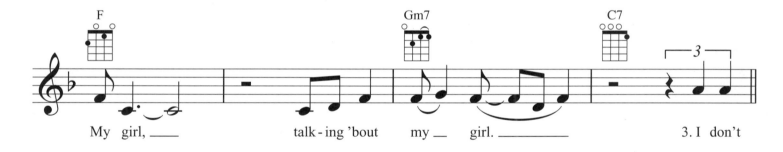

My girl, ___ talk - ing 'bout my _ girl. _____ 3. I don't

Verse

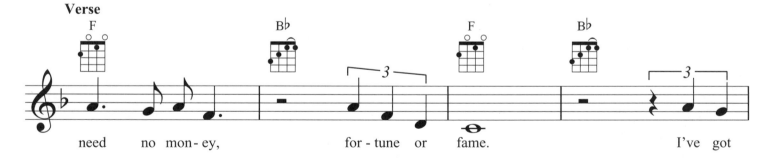

need no mon - ey, for - tune or fame. I've got

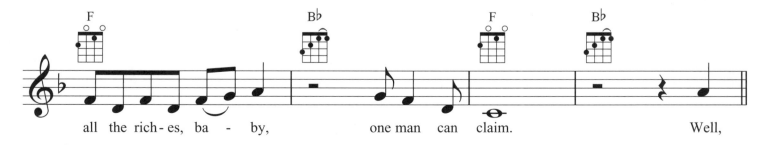

all the rich - es, ba - by, one man can claim. Well,

Chorus

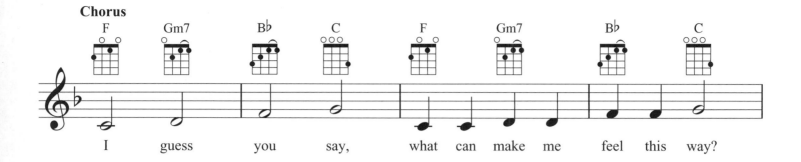

I guess you say, what can make me feel this way?

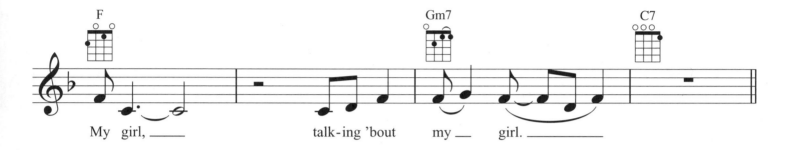

My girl, _____ talk-ing 'bout my _____ girl. _____

Outro

I've got sun-shine on a cloud - y day __ with my girl; _____ I've

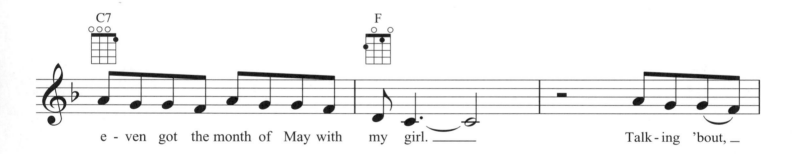

e - ven got the month of May with my girl. _____ Talk-ing 'bout, _

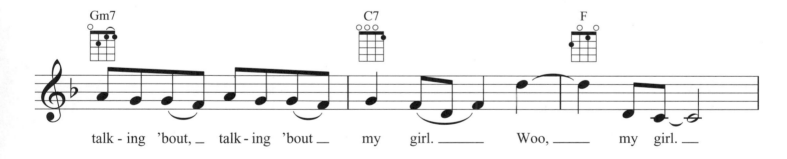

talk - ing 'bout, _ talk - ing 'bout _ my girl. _____ Woo, _____ my girl. _

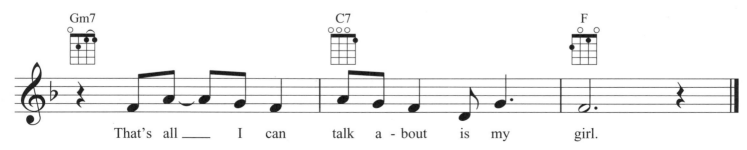

That's all _____ I can talk a - bout is my girl.

Let's Stay Together

Words and Music by Al Green, Willie Mitchell and Al Jackson, Jr.

People Get Ready

Words and Music by Curtis Mayfield

Additional Lyrics

2. So, people, get ready for the train to Jordan,
Picking up passengers coast to coast.
Faith is the key; open the doors and board 'em.
There's hope for all among those loved the most.

3. There ain't no room for the hopeless sinner
Who would hurt all mankind just to save his own.
Have pity on those whose chances grow thinner,
For there's no hiding place against the Kingdom's throne.

Stand by Me

Words and Music by Jerry Leiber, Mike Stoller and Ben E. King

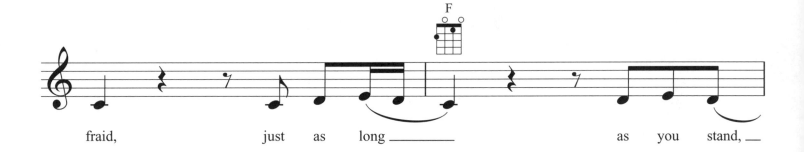

fraid,   just as long _____   as you stand, __

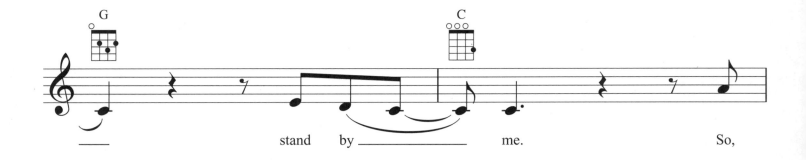

__   stand by _____ me.   So,

Chorus

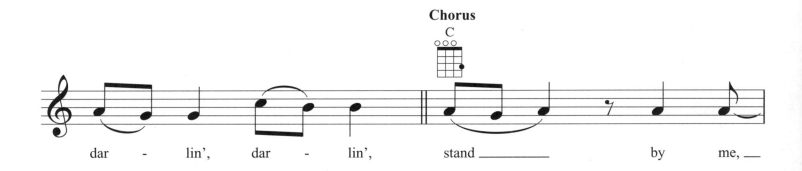

dar - lin', dar - lin',   stand _____ by me, __

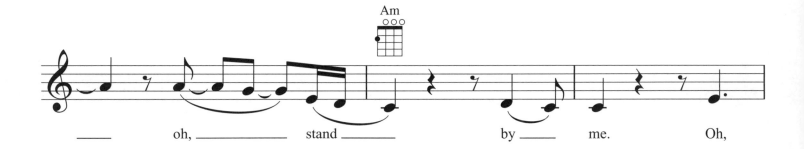

__   oh, _____ stand _____ by ____ me.   Oh,

stand, __   stand by ____ me,   stand by ____ me.

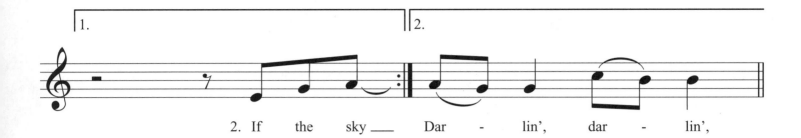

2. If the sky __ Dar - lin', dar - lin',

Outro-Chorus

stand _____ by me, _____ oh, _____ stand ____

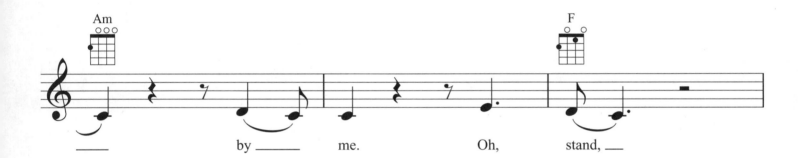

____ by ____ me. Oh, stand, __

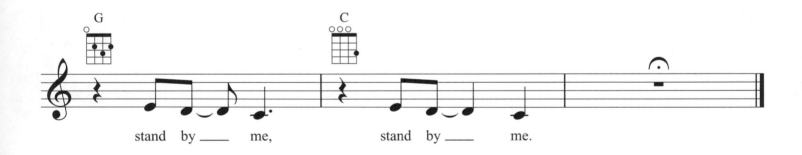

stand by __ me, stand by __ me.

Additional Lyrics

2. If the sky that we look upon should tumble and fall,
   Or the mountains should crumble to the sea,
   I won't cry, I won't cry. No, I won't shed a tear,
   Just as long as you stand, stand by me.
   And darlin', darlin'... (*To Chorus*)

Reach Out and Touch
(Somebody's Hand)

Words and Music by Nickolas Ashford and Valerie Simpson

cour - age - ment   to   some - one   who's   lost   the   way. ___   (Just
mem - ber   his   shoes   could   fit   your _ feet. ___   (Just

try.)   Or   would   I   be   talk - ing   to   a   stone   if   I   asked
try.)   Try   a   lit - tle   kind - ness   and   you'll   see   some - thing   that

you   to   share   a   prob - lem   that's   not   your   own? _____)
comes   ver - y   nat - ur - al - ly. _____)

We   can   change _ things   if   we   start   giv - ing.

Why   don't   you   reach   out   and   Why   don't   you   (Why   don't   you)

reach   out   and   touch   some - bod - y's   hand. _____

What's Love Got to Do with It

Words and Music by Graham Lyle and Terry Britten

heart can ___ be bro - ken? ___ Oh, oh. ___

I've been tak - ing on a

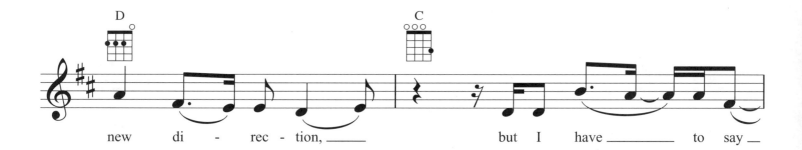

new di - rec - tion, ___ but I have ___ to say ___

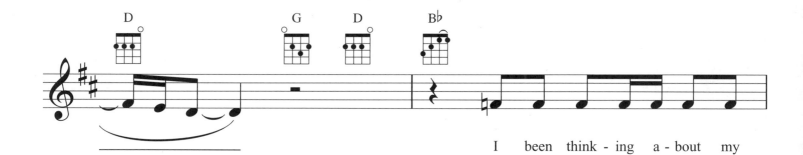

___ I been think - ing a - bout my

own pro - tec - tion. It scares me to feel this way. ___ Oh, ___

50

Chorus

Bm A G A

what's love ___ got to do, ___ got to do ___ with it?
What's love ___ got to do, ___ got to do ___ with it?

Bm A G D

What's love ___ but a sec - ond - hand e - mo - tion? ___
What's love ___ but a sweet, old - fash - ioned no - tion? ___

Bm A G A

What's love ___ got to do, ___ got to do ___ with it?

Bm A 1. G A

Who needs ___ a heart when ___ a heart can ___ be bro - ken?

2. G A Bm G Bm

heart can ___ be bro - ken?

You Can't Hurry Love

Words and Music by Edward Holland Jr., Lamont Dozier and Brian Holland

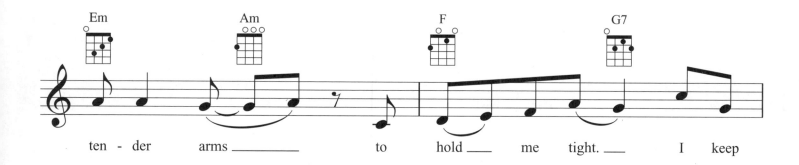

ten - der arms _____ to hold ___ me tight. ___ I keep

wait - ing; I keep on wait - ing. ___ But it ain't

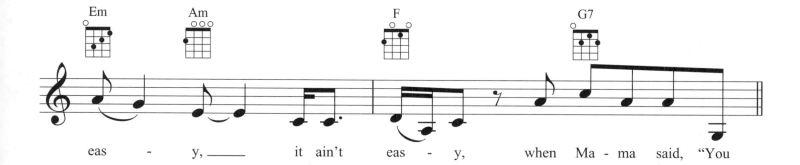

eas - y, _____ it ain't eas - y, when Ma - ma said, "You

Outro-Chorus

can't hur - ry love. ___ No, you just have to wait." She said,

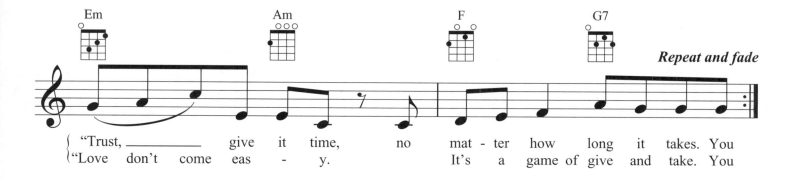

Repeat and fade

{ "Trust, _____ give it time, no mat - ter how long it takes. You
{ "Love don't come eas - y. It's a game of give and take. You

55

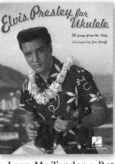